What You Said.

This fun-packed antholo[gy ...]
a gently anarchic way t[o ...]
fun at the bewildering illogicality of it all. I mean...
what crazy scheme makes 'r*ough*' sound like 'stuff'
and 'th*ough*' sound like 'tow' or even 'toe'!

But there is another, invaluable merit in this delightful collection of poems. It helps children with word strings and phonemes. To encourage their use as a teaching aid, there is a list of learning targets contained in each poem at the end of the book introduced as: *You can ignore this - it's just for TEACHERS.*

John Kitchen, Educationalist and author

I liked the poem about muddling up there, their and they're. It has really helped me to become unmuddled.   *Connor Longworth (11)*

My Cat's Groovy is funny and *Phew* helped me spell phoned. I like this book because it is very clever for using words to help you spell.

Helena Jay-Shreif (7)

Great for helping kids remember different ways of spelling the same sound.   *Year 3 Teacher*

Cold Mould helped me with my spellings a lot. I also liked the poem, *English Spelling is Bonkers,* because it is SO funny and English spelling IS bonkers! This book is not just good - it's excellent because it can teach you words the fun way.   *Lulu Jay-Shreif (8)*

Children in my class with spelling difficulties loved working with the poems, having fun reading, reciting and remembering poems and spelling patterns.
Year 6 Teacher, Bucks

I think it's a really fun way of showing imperfections in English. This is a way of making it fun, enjoyable and quite practical. I would definitely recommend this book not only to schools but to children in general. My favourite poem is *Little Cat Mabel,* making fun of the original nursery rhyme!
Joshua Severn (13)

This book would be a marvel in classrooms. The poem, *English Spelling is Bonkers,* is perfect because it covers all the spelling sounds, 'ou', 'ow', 'a', 'igh', 'ai', 'ei' and many more!   *Matty Severn (11)*

Reading *Homophone Nonsense* in class was not only enjoyable and entertaining, it also highlighted to the students how many homophones there are! Providing context to grammar is so important for learning. Love it!   *Jennifer Roberts, Year 6 Teacher*

Pob Hwyl
Gina x

ENGLISH SPELLING IS BONKERS

by

Gina Claye

© Gina Claye 2016

This book is sold subject to the condition that it shall not, by way of trade or otherwise, be lent, resold, hired out, converted to another format or otherwise circulated without the publisher's prior consent in any format other than that in which it is published.

The moral right of Gina Claye is asserted as the writer.

ISBN 978-1-910779-13-2

Typeset by Oxford eBooks Ltd.
www.oxford-ebooks.com

www.ginaclaye.co.uk

For
Nancy, Nell and Beatrice
and
all my past Year 3 students
at Monks Risborough School

Illustrations by...

Norma Straiton

Nancy Rashleigh-Claye (11)

Nell Rashleigh-Claye (8)

Beatrice Rashleigh-Claye (4)

And one or two by me...

A Bit About 'Bonkers' and Me

I started writing when I was 9 years old. I sat in the garage of my house in Ystradgynlais, South Wales and scribbled while my friends acted out what I had just written.

Many years later, I had to teach year 3 which words were spelt with 'ea' like cream and which had 'ee' like green. I wrote the poem, 'Ice cream' - much more fun than giving them a list of words to learn and so I wrote more poems ...

My good friend, Norma Straiton, agreed to do some of the illustrations and then my grandchildren, Nancy, Nell and Beatrice decided they were going to draw some too. I got hold of a pencil as well, and so it went on... and this book, 'English Spelling is Bonkers', is the result. I hope, when you read it, you pick up a few tips about spelling but most of all, I hope you find it fun!

The Poems

Guess What 1
For Sale... 2
Ship with the Sail 3
Scary Hen and the Slink Slunk Fox 4
Red Kites 6
Stork Walk... 7
English Spelling is Bonkers.............................. 8
Silent Bs 10
Cold Mould 11
My Cat's Groovy 12
How Much More? 14
Not on the Floor...15
All Aboard with Mr McCord 16
One L or Two?..18
Phew 19
Jack and Jill 20
Quarrelling with a Wasp 21
The Snowman...22
Gardening Advice 24
The Haunted Castle..25
My Mouse Called Ed.......................................26
The Monster's Head..27
Ghosts 28
Boast 29
Football Match 30
The Goat and the Stoat 32
Note..33
Little Cat Mabel 34
Mr Creepy Crawly 35
The Chocolate Bee...36
Baby Bea 37
Runny Honey 38

O U Lucky Dog 39
What and Why 40
The Getaway Train.. 41
Tick Tock Tack 42
Fashion Passion 43
Giant Black.. 44
Tough! 45
The Now Now Kids 46
The Old Cold Gnome 48
Stain On My Train 49
Barnacles on the Bottom 50
There, Their and They're.................................. 52
Homophone Nonsense 53
I Suppose 56
Thistledown... 57
Ice-cream 58
The Eleph and the Ant 59
Doesn't Fit! 60
On My Scooter 61
Mr Small 62
Did You Know? 63
Old Mrs Spider 64
The Boring Birthday 66

You Can Ignore This - It's Just For TEACHERS...... 69

Guess What

I guess...
unless
we soon have success
in finding the path we missed,
we're lost.
Don't get cross,
don't make a fuss
but if you press
me, I confess
we're in a right mess!

Next time...
Yes,
the two of us
will go by *BUS*

For Sale

The pale elephant trumpets
While the whale plays his scales
And the penguin beats a rhythm
On two stale cakes.

A little male monkey
Sings a sad tale
While the wind blows a gale
Through valley and vale.

And a lion holds a sign up saying,
'BAND FOR SALE'

this lot's spelt 'ale'

Ship with the Sail

Down pelts the rain
On the ship with the sail,
Carrying letters,
Carrying the mail.

The ship's dog
Stops wagging his tail
And the boy on deck
Bites his nails.

Down thunders the hail,
Down without fail,
As the ship lists sideways
The boy grabs the rail.

A wail from the captain
But I only laugh...
*Cos it's not on the sea
It's in my bath!*

and this lot's 'ail'

Scary Hen and the Slink Slunk Fox

Round the farmyard barn
In the middle of the night
When the moon was full
And shining bright,

A fox slink slunk,
His paws so light,
Crept up to the hens
Who clucked in fright.

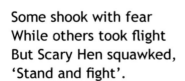

Some shook with fear
While others took flight
But Scary Hen squawked,
'Stand and fight'.

She pecked him on the left paw
Then the right,
She bit his tail
And held on tight.

The fox he pulled
With all his might
Till his tail dropped off,
A sorry plight!

Squawked Scary Hen
'Get going, left, right',
And the fox slink slunk
Till he was out of sight.

that's RIGHT —
they're all spelt
'ight'

Red Kites

I was flying my kite
At quite a height ←
When a bird took a bite
From my red and white kite.

She pecked out the white bits,
Flashed her forked tail
Then the two red kites
Away they sailed.

If they hadn't stuck an 'e' in, it could have gone in the Scary Hen poem

a red kite is a bird of prey with a forked tail – go on, look them up

Stork Walk

I went for a walk
And near a dandelion stalk
I found a piece of chalk
That began to talk

It said in a funny sort of way

'I'm not going to draw a fork
I'm not going to draw a cork
I'm going to draw a big bird, a stork

And then I'm going to fly away.'

English Spelling is Bonkers

In the morning you're yawning
Though you know you'll go out with Joe
Whose whacky scarf is a laugh
    and a half.

This verse gets worse
As you burst with thirst
Cos at one you ate a bun
    that weighs a ton.

At the zoo at two
Feeling blue through and through
Cos fleas nipped your knees
    if you please.

At four you roar
You can't take any more,
You fly right home
    for a bite.

a right mixture !

At eight you go straight
To the fete and wait
For your mate, it's great...
    I don't think so!

I ask you...
English spelling is
BONKERS!

Silent Bs

I like bees
Noisy buzzy bees
But I don't like the kind
Which are silent

Climb and crumb
Comb and thumb
Limb and lamb
And numb ... it's dumb!

Cold Mould

Don't you think... that ALL words
That rhyme with old
Should be spelt like old?
Like this...

This ice cube's cold,
It's freezing to hold,
Okay - I'll do as I'm told,
No need to scold!

But no, just take a look
At this lot...

At cricket you're bowled,
Old cheese has mould,
The mare has foaled
And my Dad has doled
Out the chocolates...
And mine have rolled
Onto the floor!

You're right...
English Spelling is Bonkers!

My Cat's Groovy

My cat's groovy,
Real choosy,
Thinks the sun's dumb.
Afternoons
He should be snoozing
On the shed roof
But when it hots up
He gets up
And zooms in
Out of the blue
For a quick kip.

But at night
The cat flap flips
And out he slips,
Moves smoothly
Over leaves and roots,
Shoots up the shed roof,
Grooms ears and neck,
Broods,
Lazily eyes his territory
Then lies back
And moonbathes.

2 words are NOT ALLOWED in the choosy, groovy 'oo' gang though they sound the same – can you spy them?

My cat's groovy,
Dead choosy,
In fact
He's quite
A cool cat.

hope he doesn't catch the 'flu' !

How Much More?

How much more
needs to pour
out of this tap, before
the sink fills
and the water spills
all over the floor?

4 different ways of ~~spilling~~ spelling one sound...

And can I do it before
my sister, who's only four,
bursts through the door
and starts to roar
for mum to come.

Not on the Floor

I'm jumping around on the table,
Was that the cloth that tore?
Before Mum comes in from the garden
I'll be a fierce lion, *ROAR*.

I've run lots of laps round the table,
I didn't quite keep the score,
Whoops, there goes the teapot   ... *and here!*
And the milk and the mugs – all four.

Mum's hurrying in from the garden,
Oh dear, it's beginning to pour,
Sorry Mum, I know it's wrong, but...
I was ever so bored with the floor.

All Aboard with Mr McCord

Reports just now are flying in
    that cannot be ignored
of that ancient rusty rocket,
    built by old Mr McCord.

'score' – and ANOTHER 3 ways of spelling the 'ore' bit.

He's torn out the worn out engine,
    put in weird gadgets galore,
dusted the rust off with custard
    ready to set off and explore.

It's powered by stale cream crackers
    and baked beans by the score
with splinters of banana skins
    and the juice of an apple core.

It's plastered with sonic Smarties
    from the ceiling to the floor
with an upside down umbrella
    in case it starts to pour.

He's painted all the portholes
    has old Mr McCord
with the tastiest chunkiest marmalade
    that he could afford.

Before the lollipops are loaded
    and the chocolate ice cream stored
he orders his crew, four spiders,
    'Scurry up there, crawl aboard.

Ready at last for blast off
    it totters back and fore
then rockets off into orbit
    with a whooshing, rushing roar.

They say it's ace at crash landing,
    I won't say any more,
But, *Get Ready, Take Cover...*
    It might land at your door.

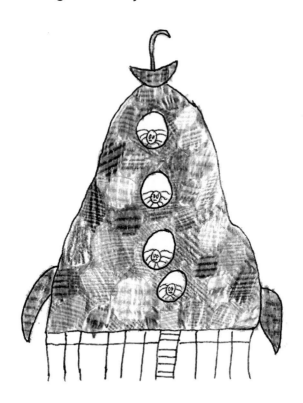

One L or Two?

I've already had
    one mouthful
which feels like
    one bucketful
I can't eat any more, not even
    one mouthful

I'm... *two* (whoops, sorry!) too full up!

WHY can't they stick to ONE?

Phew

An elephant and her nephew
Came to call on me,
They ate my alphabet letters,
My phrase book and phonics for tea.

They phoned a friend then vanished,
Were they phantoms or really there?
But I've taken a photo to prove it
And there's a pile of pooh on the stair.

Phew, I'm glad they've gone I admit it,
Hope they weren't sick from the tea
And I'll get the paddling pool ready...
In case a dolphin calls on me.

how many words with
'ph' can you ~~phind~~ find?

Jack and Jill

'Jack and Jill
You're not up the hill
Filling your pail
Of water!'

'Don't be silly
It's far too chilly
To climb up the hill
For water.'

'If you're thirsty still
We certainly will
Turn on the tap
For water.'

Quarrelling with a Wasp

Never quarrel with a wasp,
You might want to wallop it,
You might try to squash it
Or wash it away
With Mum's hosepipe.

What did I tell you,
Was it yesterday?

They want an 'o' sound so they write 'a' – Bonkers!

Don't quarrel with a wasp,
You don't have a magic wand
To wave it away
So... leg it like lightning
And in future Watch Out!

The Snowman

One winter morning
     in the cold and the sleet,
a snowman was snoozing
     and dreamt he'd grown feet.

He paced to and fro,
     did a rock 'n a roll,
ripped the clothes off the line
     and slid down the pole.

*'ow' sound –
5 different ways
of spelling it...*

He jumped onto the wheelbarrow
     which broke with a crack,
He tumbled right over
     and fell on his back.

'Whoops a daisy,' said the sparrow,
     'Told you so,' cried the crow,
'Keep on going,' said red robin
     as he swooped down low.

But the snowman just lay there
     with the icy winds blowing,
all around him
     snowing and snowing.

He sat up at last
     and groaned, 'I suppose
the problem with feet is
     on the end you've got toes.

'How I'm suffering
   nobody knows,
MY FEET ARE FREEZING
   AND MY TOES ARE FROZE.'

With that he woke up,
   no feet could he see,
He was still where they'd built him
   by the old oak tree.

A smile spread slowly
   over his face,
cos he was stuck
   firmly in place.

It lit up his eyes
   and his carroty nose
cos he didn't have feet
   and he didn't have toes.

Gardening Advice

For a spot of quick gardening
Choose a dry day and...

Plant a flower that's a fast grower
(In a shower you'd be slower)
To keep your tower of grass lower
Get a power mower

if it sounds different WHY do they spell it THE SAME WAY !!

The Haunted Castle

If you go to the castle
   Tiptoe with care
For they say it is haunted
   And nothing lives there.

The door slams behind you,
   Look round if you dare,
You hear the bolt rattle
   But nothing is there.

A sigh from the landing,
   A quick creak of a chair,
You shiver and tremble
   But nothing is there.

It's brushing your cheek,
   It's lifting your hair,
You peep through your fingers
   But nothing is there.

Nothing is watching
   As you start up the stair,
You may think you're alone
   But Nothing is there.

Turn back now, go home
   As a moaning you hear
Or *NOTHING* will get you
   For *NOTHING* waits there.

*beware there
on the stair !*

My Mouse Called Ed

I put a mouse
In my mum's bed,
She yelled and yelled
And away it fled.

It ran past the dog
Whose name was Fred
Who barked and barked
Cos he hadn't been fed.

Then Dad cut his finger
Which bled and bled
And turned all the cornflakes
Red, bright red.

I quickly picked him up
My mouse called Ed
And put him back safely
In the garden shed.

you SAY bed, you SPELL it bed...

The Monster's Head

I found a monster recipe book
  And this is what I read,
If you want a monster sandwich
  You need a monster's head.

Boil it till it's inside out,
  Hold the saucepan steady,
Take it out, shake upside down
  Until it's good and ready.

Mash it up with strawberry jam,
  (Take out its teeth of lead),
If oozy bits drip on the floor
  Be careful where you tread.

Stick the monster mixture
  Between two chunks of bread,
If you want a filling sandwich
  Make sure it's thickly spread.

But looking at this monster snack
  Fills me with such dread,
I think I'll just pop down the shop
  And buy some crisps instead.

... so WHY add an 'a'?

Can't catch me!

Ghosts

I posted an invite to Charlie
For the party I love the most,
On Hallowe'en night
We got such a fright
For the rest of the guests were ghosts.

Boast

We boasted we'd have the best banquet
At our barbecue down by the coast,
But the beef burger van
Got stuck in the sand
So all we could roast was toast.

they've stuck in an 'a' again ...

Football Match

OUR TEAM
Best you ever saw,
We're not going to lose,
It's against the law.
Their team's boring
Yawn, yawn,
We'll make them wish
They'd never been born.

It's a disaster,
Their team's scored,
We boohed
Their fans roared.
We want a goal
Come on sport,
Ace or penalty
Any sort.

YEAH GOAL!
Now it's a draw,
Poor old goalie's
On the floor.
Come on team
Give it your all,
Two minutes more
And we've got the ball...

*it's 'aw', 'or' and 'a' (again)
but who cares, it's
FOOTBALL ...*

IT'S IN THE NET
WHAM, YEAH!
Ref's blown the whistle
We yell and cheer.
We've taught them a lesson
Hear us scream,
IT'S A WIN FOR
OUR HOME TEAM!

The Goat and the Stoat

I rowed my old boat
round the castle moat,
'Can I come too?'
asked the goat
in a coat.

Only if you can float...

I rowed with the goat
round the castle moat
'Can I come too?'
asked the stoat
with a sore throat.

Only if you can float...

With the goat and the stoat
I rowed my old boat
while the hole in the bottom
got bigger and bigger

Till the goat and the stoat
fell out of the boat...
And we all had to float
round the castle moat.

*at least they're
ALL the same – 'oat'...*

Note

I voted
YES...
Let me
quote you
what I wrote
and note this,
I voted
YES
To DO AWAY
with school dinners !!

... except for these !

Little Cat Mabel

Little cat Mabel
Stood on the table
Eyeing a good fish pie,
She put up her paw
And pulled out each claw,
Took a quick look,
No sign of the cook,
Hooked all the fish
Right out of the dish...
And said, 'What a full puss am I.'

good ... WHY can't they just write gud?

Mr Creepy Crawly

Early in the morning
   At the crack of dawn,
Mr Creepy Crawly
   Was crawling on the lawn.

He crawled up a daisy
   And under a log
Then he crawled a little further
   And what do you think he saw?

A great fierce cat
   With very sharp claws,
Watching him and waiting
   With wide open jaws.

Mr Creepy Crawly
   Curled into a ball
And he rolled and he rolled
   Far away from her paws.

'aw', glad it got away

The Chocolate Bee

Can you see
that chocolate bee
hanging on
my Christmas tree

Can you see
that chocolate bee
lift his wings
and fly away free

Baby Bea

Baby Bea
went to sea
to catch some fish
for her tea

Baby Bea
ate her tea
five fish fingers
and one green pea

this time the 'a' has
KICKED OUT one of the 'e's

Runny Honey

My nose is very runny,
That's quite funny
cos it's not cold it's sunny,
Ugh Nasty Nose, Yucky!

Can I have money
to buy some honey?
Oh No Eating's Yucky!

Beatrice, aged 4, wanted to do the
illustrations too ... so I gave her a pencil ...

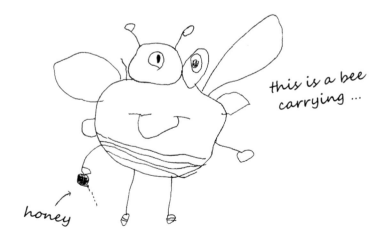

this is a bee carrying ...

honey

O U Lucky Dog

o u lucky dog
Could you please lie down
o u lucky dog
You really *should* lie down
o u lucky dog
Would you PLEASE lie down

If you don't
You won't
Get this bone!

What and Why

Whisker, whisper
Whistle, whale
All have silent 'h'
Without fail

Whiz, whisk, whirl
Whip, whop, whack
All have silent 'h'
That's a fact

What, when, where
Which, white, while
All have silent 'h'
Why oh why?

It's got into school too

The Getaway Train

The getaway train sped along on the rails
With a hiss in its voice and a scowl on its face,
'I don't want to work, I just want to play,
Want to sail on the ship that lies in the bay,
    Got to get away, got to get away.'

The getaway train ran off the rails,
Waved to the ship and gave a loud hail,
'Have you room for a train, just a wee little space
To carry me off to a faraway place?
    Got to get away, got to get away.'

The station master gazed at the rails,
Shook his watch, his face very grave,
'That train's overdue, it's half past eight,
I want my supper, don't want to wait,
    Got to get away, got to get away.'

The getaway train stood near the ship's rails
With a boom in its voice and smile on its face,
'I'll breathe fresh air and salt sea spray
And sit in the sun and play all day,
    Now I've got away, I've got away.'

Tick Tock Tack

Tick tock tack
Sick sock sack
Curly c and kicking k
Stick stock stack

Lick lock luck
Mick mock muck
Curly c and kicking k
Click clock cluck

Fashion Passion

Hattie my cat
Has a passion
For fashion
She wears a bonnet
With a bow on it
I must ration
Her passion
For tuck
Or her ears
Will get stuck

Giant Black

Giant Black
ran down the track,
a wriggling sack
upon his back.

Down with a whack
he fell, smack,
the sack went crack
and out jumped Jack.

Tough!

Can I do it?

I've read it through
And it's tough
Enough
Without my feeling thoroughly
Rough
Cos of my cough.

Ought to have a go though,
Better settle down and plough
On...
With this horrid homework!

7 DIFFERENT ways of saying 'OUGH'. I despair!

The Now Now Kids

We're the Now Now kids
Want everything NOW,
Won't wait a second
We vow, man, vow.
Want a bag of crisps,
Plenty in the house,
Fingers in the cupboard,
Quiet as a mouse.

Want a computer
Hear us howl,
Gotta wait till Christmas,
Scowl, man, scowl.
Want to fly an aeroplane
Upside down,
Want to zoom a racing car
Right round town.

Told we're too young
There's no doubt,
Get so frustrated
We shout, man, shout
We're the Now Now kids
Want everything NOW,
Won't wait a second
We vow, man, vow.

So we want to be older,
Yes, and how!
Want to be grown up
NOW RIGHT NOW

*'ow', 'ou', 'o'
all sounding the
same – can you
SPOT them?*

The Old Cold Gnome

In the woods it was cold,
very cold,
so I told
the gnome, the old
old gnome to fold
his beard and hold
it round his cold,
cold tummy.

He gave me a bold,
bold grin
and a bag of gold
which I sold
for something yummy
to put in my hungry,
hungry tummy.

Stain On My Train

That pigeon's
Done a stain
On my new train
I hope the rain
Will wash it off

It's such a pain
My brand new train
If he does it again
I'll *SQUASH* him off

Barnacles on the Bottom

The fishing boat lay on his side in the mud,
'I won't go to sea,' he cried,
'Don't try to tow me, don't try to scold me,
I feel old and cold and tired.'
The fisherman sighed, and stroked his beard
And said, 'I'm afraid you've got 'em,
It's what I feared, slime on the sides
And barnacles on the bottom.'

> But the boat moaned and the boat groaned
> 'I won't go, I told you so,
> No, no, no, no, NO!'

The fisherman chuckled, 'You're not finished yet,
Though you moan that you're tired and cold,
I know once you're sailing, you'll show you're not ailing
And prove you're not feeble and old.
But first we must rub you and scour you and scrub you
And rip out the rope that's rotten
And scrape off the slithering slime on the sides
And barnacles on the bottom.'

> But the boat moaned and the boat groaned
> 'I won't go, I told you so,
> No, no, no, no, NO!'

Lots of words! can you FISH OUT the ones with 'oa', 'ow', 'o-e', and 'o'?

When all was shipshape, they got him afloat
And they fished from river to coast,
They netted all floaters, both sardines and bloaters
And brought home a catch fit to roast.
He sailed all day long, with a grin not a groan
Until he had quite forgotten,
He'd felt old and tired with slime on the side
And barnacles on the bottom.

    And the boat rocked and the boat rolled
    'There's no one at sea quite like me
    No, no, no, no,
    NO!

There, Their and They're

There is, quite near my foot
a spider,
There's another one
beside her.

Their legs are
sprawling and hairy,
Their eyes are
sinister and scary.

They're staring at me
and that's not all,
They're starting to crawl
towards me……….. *YIKES !*

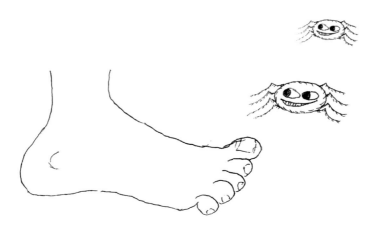

Homophone Nonsense

Nancy, my granddaughter, was doing homophones in Year 6 so we put our heads together and came up with this ...

One night, a knight of old
Trod on a pane of glass
In his bare feet. Crack!
He nearly hit the ceiling
The pain was so hard to bear.
I must write, he thought,
To let my mum know
There's no need to worry,
I'm as right as rain.

He sealed the letter
With sealing wax,
Rode along the road
Through driving rain,
Reined in his horse
And threw his mum's letter
Into the letter box.

Meanwhile his mum was in Wales
Searching for dolphins and whales
'The sea is calm,' she wails,
'But I can't see a thing.'

Homophones – words sounding the same but spelt differently

She read his letter,
It made her see red,
'Get to hospital,' she cried,
'They'll heal your heel.'

She won the day, the knight
Hobbled to hospital on one leg,
'There's a hole in your heel,
You'll stay here for a whole week,'
Said the nurse, 'Do you hear me!'

They bandaged him up
And put him to bed,
They fed him coarse fish
Which he hated of course
And plain hicabo cheese
Which they flew in by plane.

After a plateful of rotten plaice
The knight wondered whether
He would ever escape
from that dreadful place
The weather turned cold
The wind blew and blew
And turned his toes blue.

At last they allowed him
To leave. He shouted aloud,
'I'm free, I'm free!
I'm feeling weak
But I'm sure in a week
I'll be ok, just you see.'

The maid made him a cake
With a flower on top
From stale yucky flour,
He ate a piece of the
Disgusting cake, just
In order to keep the peace.
He ate eight bananas
Followed by cereal
Then watched on TV
His favourite serial.

When his mother returned,
She cried, 'My son,
I must keep an eye on you,
You will stay by my side
Come rain or sunshine,
We will buy a farm
With a pig in a sty
And to knightly adventures
You can say
Bye bye!'

I Suppose

My dad goes
outside
and shows me
how he gets rid
of the crows
with the garden hose

I suppose
if I sniff that
highly scented rose
my nose will itch
and my toes twitch

Today
I chose
to go inside,
before I got frozen,
for a doze
zzzzzzZZZZZZZZZZZ

*how many words rhyme
with CROWS – are they
all spelt the same way?*

Thistledown

Fairies,
Stealing away on the breeze,
Seek an earthling bed
For winter, to nestle in.
They sleep there unseen
Till the beams of the spring sun
Wake them from their dreaming.

Once white winged, now
Green sheathed, they lift
Their faces secretly
To the summer sun,
Revealing,
In the scheme of things,
The unceasing magic of the seasons.

there are 15 WORDS with an 'ee' sound with 5 DIFFERENT spellings – can you find them?

Ice-cream

I like ice-cream,
I eat it on my cheese,
I mix it with my marmalade
And spoon it on my peas.

I always take a little lick
When Mum is watching me
But I take a slurp, a great big slurp
When no one's there to see.

I roll it slowly round my tongue,
It slides from cheek to cheek
And when at last I swallow it
It makes my stomach freeze.

I like it when it's strawberry pink
And minty green's a treat
With little bits of chocolate
That crunch between my teeth.

When asked if I have had enough
On eating two or three,
I always say, in a hopeful way
'Lots more ice-cream, please!'

Can you think of any MORE words spelt like CREAM and GREEN ?

The Eleph and the Ant

An unhappy tearful Eleph
Stood in the mud and pined,
'The front of me's feeling all cut off,
It's lonely without a behind.'

It tried pinching the end from a curr***,
The beginning from a tired ***elope,
The middle from p***ts and S***a
But they all whipped them back at a stroke.

Its tears dripped down on a notice
With WANTED in letters of red,
All the jungle were there to toast them
When the eleph and ant were W   ED.

Doesn't Fit!

Fill, fell, full
They all have double ll
Bill, bell, bull
Double ll as well

Fill, fell, full
They all have double ll
Will, well, wool ...?
Wool doesn't fit
Not one bit
Two round OOs
And just one L

On My Scooter

I'm skimming along on my scooter,
    Into the park, toot, toot,
There's a big fat pigeon blocking my path,
    Out of my way, you brute.

I shoot past a coot on the duck pond,
    Past Granny in a red tracksuit,
I wave to three girls strumming guitars
    And a boy who is playing the flute.

I swerve in and out of the swings
    Past the roundabout and half an old boot,
I lift up my scooter, whiz up the steps
    And free wheel with ease down the chute.

Whoops, I nearly ran over that cat
    With a monster of a dog in pursuit,
Watch out, whew, just missed that tree
    And its bit of great sticking out root.

This scooting is making me hungry
    Though I do have a piece of old fruit,
But I can't help feeling a bit fed up
    Cos there's no ice-cream van on this route.

Lots of words rhyme with 'toot' BUT don't have 'oo'

Mr Small

There's a very small
Creature creeping
Up the wall,
It isn't very long,
And it isn't very tall.

It feels very furry,
It's as round as a ball
And it's hanging on tight
In case it should fall.

I think Dad would like to see it,
I'll give him a call,
I haven't seen one like this
Before at all.

Did You Know?

Did you know…

Knights of old
knocked on doors
till their knuckles
were knackered?

Knitted knickers
tickle?

You can use a knife
to cut a knob of butter
But it's much more fun
to kneel on it
and squash it flat
with your knees

You knew that
didn't you…

Old Mrs Spider

A flighty young fly got caught in a web,
   'My supper,' smiled old Mrs Spider,
'This blackberry bush is a fine place to be,'
   And she wove her web wider and wider.

'You're a nice fat prize,' she said with delight,
   'And my scheme you have to admire,
Flies like blackberries and I like flies,'
   And she wound her web higher and higher.

'You let me go,' cried the frightened young fly,
   Adding 'please', which is much politer,
But sly Mrs Spider just licked her lips
   And twined the threads tighter and tighter.

Then the sky grew dark and the rain poured down
   And the wind blew mightier and mightier,
A blackberry dropped, and plopped through the web
   As the lightning flashed brighter and brighter.

Old Mrs Spider clung to a leaf
   With her torn web tattered beside her,
And the fly winked his eye, as he waved her goodbye,
   'No supper tonight, Mrs Spider.'

BELIEVE IT OR NOT, there are 7 different ways of spelling the 'i' sound (spider) in this poem — found them?

The Boring Birthday

OK, you've done all the HARD work — this is just for FUN !

It was a very boring birthday
The day that I was eight,
An elephant crashed down the street
And pounded through my gate.

He thundered down the garden path,
Squeezed through the patio door,
Trod on my brand new roller skates
And skidded round the floor.

He didn't have an invite
To come to my birthday tea,
So I didn't offer him one of my crisps
When he sat down next to me.

He splattered the banana ice-cream,
Made the strawberry jelly quake
And blasted off the candles
On my spaceship birthday cake.

He whopped and walloped the sausages
In a tomato ketchup mess,
Guzzled the mish mash and blew it back out
All down my sister's dress.

He twirled a bowl of trifle
And aimed for my brother's head
But missed and a dollop of custard
Walloped the cat instead.

I yawned and went on munching
As he left with a piled up plate,
It was a very boring birthday
The day that I was eight.

You Can Ignore This – It's Just For TEACHERS

a(wash) *Quarrelling with a Wasp*

a(Santa, wanted) *The Eleph and the Ant*

ai(train), ay(day), a-e(face), eigh(eight)
The Getaway Train

ail(sail) *Ship with the Sail*

ale(sale) *For Sale*

ain(rain) *Stain on my Train*

air(stair), are(care), ere(there) *The Haunted Castle*

alk(talk), ork(fork) *Stork Walk*

all(wall) *Mr Small*

ashion(fashion), assion(passion), ation(ration)
Fashion Passion

aw(paw) *Mr Creepy Crawly*

aw(law), a(ball), or(born) *Football Match*

ea(tea) *Baby Bea*

ee(tree) *The Chocolate Bee*

ead(head) *The Monster's Head*

ed(red) *My Mouse called Ed*

ee(breeze), ea(beams), e(secretly), e-e(scheme),
ie(fairies) *Thistledown*

ee(green), ea(treat), e(me) *Ice cream*

final 'ck' *Tick Tock Tack, Giant Black*

final 'l'(mouthful), 'll'(full), *One or Two, Doesn't Fit!*

final 'll'(hill) Jack and Jill

final 'ss'(mess), 's'(bus) *Guess What*

homophones *Homophone Nonsense*

i-e(smile), ie(flies), igh(high), eye(eye), y(fly),
ye(goodbye), I (I) *Old Mrs Spider*

ight(night) *Scary Hen and the Slink Slunk Fox*

ite(kite), eight(height) *Red Kites*

oaled(foaled), old(cold), oled(doled), olled(rolled),
ould(mould), owled(bowled) *Cold Mould*

oar(roar), oor(floor), ore(more), our(pour)
*How Much More? Not on the Floor,
All Aboard With Mr McCord*

oast(boast) *Boast*

ost(most) *Ghosts*

oat(boat) *The Goat and the Stoat*

ote(vote) *Note*

old(cold) *The Old Cold Gnome*

oo(roof), o-e(move), ue(blue) *My Cat's Groovy*

oo(good), u(full) *Little Cat Mabel*

oot(boot), uit(suit), ute(flute), oute(route)
On My Scooter

oney(honey), unny(funny) *Runny Honey*

ose(rose), ows(crows), oes(goes), oze(doze) *I Suppose*

ough(rough, cough, though, plough, thoroughly,
through, ought) *Tough*

ould(could) *O U Lucky Dog*

ow(snow), oa(oak), o-e(rope), o(roll), oe(toes)
The Snowman

70

ow(tow), oa(moan), o-e(rope), o(cold)
  Barnacles on the Bottom

ow(town), ou(shout) *The Now Now Kids*

ower(flower, grower) *Gardening Advice*

ph(phone) *Phew*

right old mixture! *English Spelling is Bonkers*

silent 'b' *Silent Bs*

silent 'h' *What and Why*

silent 'k' *Did You Know?*

there, their, they're *There, Their and They're*

verbs, interesting ones - and just for fun!
  The Boring Birthday

72

Lightning Source UK Ltd.
Milton Keynes UK
UKOW02f1621210616

276789UK00001B/6/P